CAMAROS

By Heather Moore Niver

Gareth Stevens
Publishing

Please visit our Web site, www.garethstevens.com. For a free color catalog of all our high-quality books, call toll free 1-800-542-2595 or fax 1-877-542-2596.

Library of Congress Cataloging-in-Publication Data

Niver, Heather Moore.
 Camaros / Heather Moore Niver.
     p. cm. – (Wild wheels)
 Includes index.
 ISBN 978-1-4339-4736-0 (pbk.)
 ISBN 978-1-4339-4737-7 (6-pack)
 ISBN 978-1-4339-4735-3 (library binding)
 1. Camaro automobile–History–Juvenile literature. I. Title.
 TL215.C33N58 2011
 629.222'2–dc22

                                    2010032883

First Edition

Published in 2011 by
Gareth Stevens Publishing
111 East 14th Street, Suite 349
New York, NY 10003

Copyright © 2011 Gareth Stevens Publishing

Designer: Christopher Logan
Editor: Therese Shea

Photo credits: Cover, p. 1 (Camaro) Photos.com/Thinkstock; cover, pp. 1, 2–3 (background), 30–32 (background), back cover (engine), 1, 2–32 (flame border), 8–9, 11, 14–15, 16, 17, 24–25, 26–27, 27 (inset), 28–29, Shutterstock.com; pp. 4–5, 12–13, 18–19, 22–23 © Kimball Stock Photo; pp. 5, 7 (inset), 10 iStockphoto.com; pp. 6–7, 9 (inset) Car Culture/Getty Images; pp. 20–21, 29 Rusty Jarrett/Getty Images for NASCAR; p. 21 (inset) Sam Greenwood/Getty Images; p. 23 (inset) Brian Cleary/AFP/Getty Images; p. 25 Brendan Hoffman/Getty Images.

Printed in the United States of America

CPSIA compliance information: Batch #CW11GS: For further information contact Gareth Stevens, New York, New York at 1-800-542-2595.

CONTENTS

Words in the glossary appear in **bold** type the first time they are used in the text.

Classic and Cutting Edge

Chevrolet is a brand in the General Motors (GM) family of cars. If you're a car fan, you've probably heard of the Chevrolet, or "Chevy," Camaro. The Camaro is a stylish, affordable car. From the first model more than 40 years ago to its most current **design**, the Camaro has enjoyed great popularity. Perhaps your parents or grandparents drove one!

The stripes down the hood of this 1969 Camaro are sometimes called "rally stripes."

New Camaros speed down U.S. highways today. People still restore, or fix up, older Camaro models to rumble down the road. All car fans should know something about the history of this classic American car.

INSIDE THE MACHINE

There are different models, or kinds, of Camaros. The Camaro Z28 was built to race in the Trans Am sedan series of the Sports Car Club of America (SCCA). It had a platform (or size, power, and design) called an "F-body." This was the same platform used for the Pontiac Firebird, another GM car.

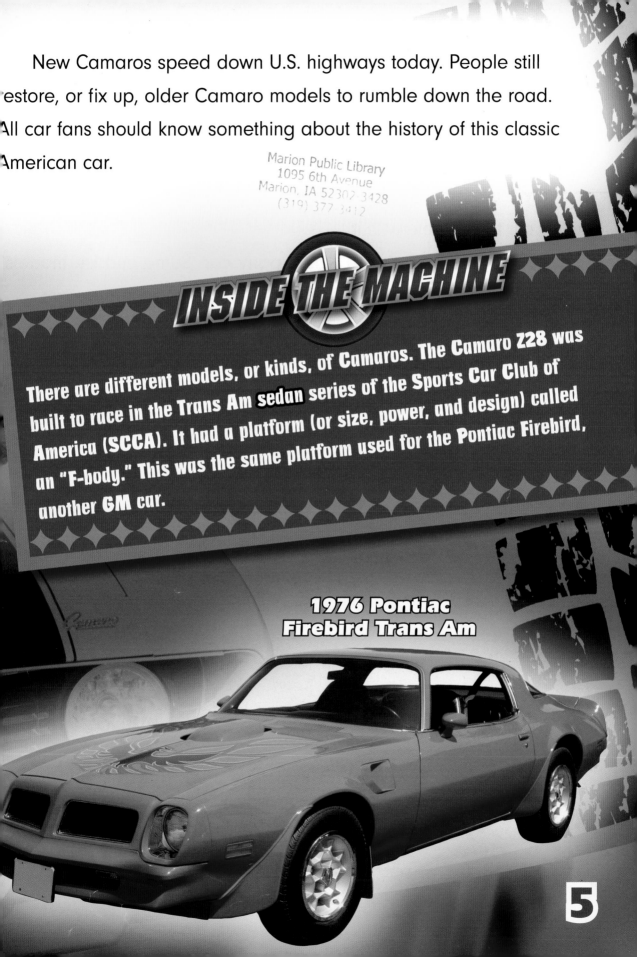

1976 Pontiac Firebird Trans Am

Chasing the Mustang

In 1967, the Chevy Camaro raced into—and out of—car showrooms. The first Camaro was built after the Ford Motor Company produced its wildly successful Mustang. GM quickly realized that they needed a similar car to compete with it.

Like its rival, the Camaro was a **pony car**. Some midsize models were called **muscle cars.** Camaros were also called sports cars. One of the first Camaros was a **pace car** in the 1967 Indianapolis 500! Others thought they were for long, relaxed drives. The Camaro was a car for everyone!

INSIDE THE MACHINE

Chevrolet said that the name "Camaro" was based on the French word for "friend." Some said Ford Motor Company workers found a meaning similar to a shrimp-like animal. Chevy workers joked back that it was named after a small, mean animal that eats Ford Mustangs!

1967 Ford Mustang GT

The Camaro was created using the same basic body as some other GM cars.

7

Early Models (1967–1969)

The first generation, or class, of Camaros was modeled after the new Chevy Nova design of 1968. It was only available as a **coupe** or **convertible**. The next year, Chevy gave the car special **shocks** that helped the driver speed up smoothly, especially on bumpy roads.

The 1969 Camaro—considered by some car fans to be the greatest year for the Camaro—had a much sportier look. It had a new **grille**, **fenders**, and taillights. The '69 Camaro also had a much more angled appearance than earlier Camaros, which were smooth and rounded.

Pony cars like the Camaro are known for their long hoods.

The 1968 Camaro was the first to have cloth seats with a black-and-white houndstooth pattern. The next year, the model known as the Camaro SS/RS convertible had seats covered in orange and black houndstooth. "SS" stands for Super Sport. "RS" stands for Rally Sport.

houndstooth pattern

Second Generation (1970 – 1981)

The next generation of Camaros went on the market in 1970. Chevy decided that bigger and heavier was better for these Camaros. Although this model had a sleeker body and better **suspension**, the design generally stayed the same. Then, in 1978, Chevrolet changed the design. The Camaro had a new front, or nose, with big bumpers under soft plastic.

Chevrolet has produced five generations of Camaros so far.

In 1980 and 1981, Chevy made Camaros that used less gas. However, the less-powerful engines in these cars made them unpopular with speed-loving drivers. The 1981 model hardly changed from 1980. It was the last model year for the second generation.

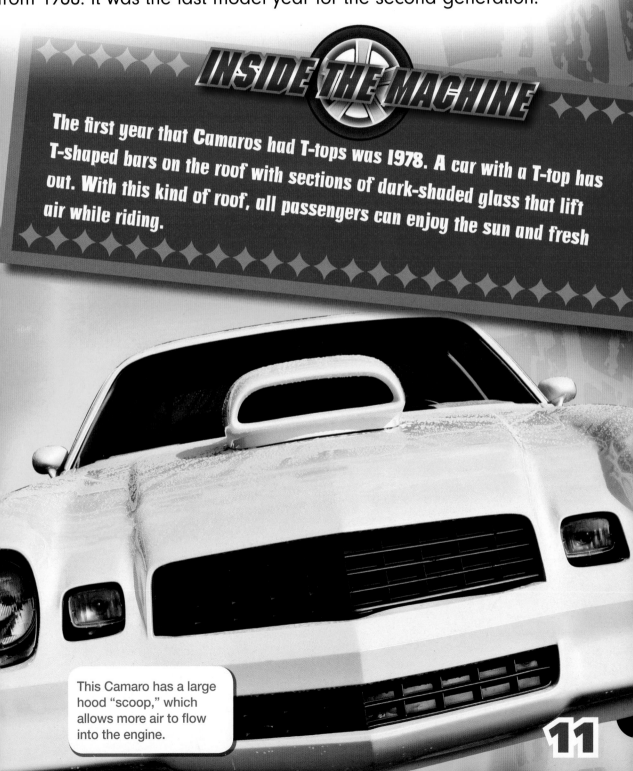

INSIDE THE MACHINE

The first year that Camaros had T-tops was 1978. A car with a T-top has T-shaped bars on the roof with sections of dark-shaded glass that lift out. With this kind of roof, all passengers can enjoy the sun and fresh air while riding.

This Camaro has a large hood "scoop," which allows more air to flow into the engine.

11

Third Generation (1982 – 1992)

General Motors started their third generation of Camaros with an all-new car—from engine to frame. It was slightly smaller than the earlier models.

In 1985, the Camaro known as the IROC-Z came on the scene. Named after the famous International Race of Champions (IROC), it turned heads with its 16-inch (41-cm) wheels. It also had one-of-a-kind decals, or stickers. That same year, *Car and Driver* magazine put the IROC-Z on its Ten Best list. The Z28 was introduced in 1990, but some car fans said that it wasn't much different from an IROC-Z.

INSIDE THE MACHINE

A convertible car is also known as a "ragtop" because the roof is cloth. In 1987, the Camaro ragtop returned for the first time since 1969. It would disappear again in 1993, only to reappear in 1994. After another discontinuation, Camaro fans were happy to hear the news of a 2011 Camaro convertible.

The 1989 Camaro IROC-Z was offered as a convertible.

Fourth Generation (1993 – 2002)

Once again, the fourth generation started out with a new design, but it didn't have as many major changes as the third generation. The front fenders were plastic, and the body sported a slick new style.

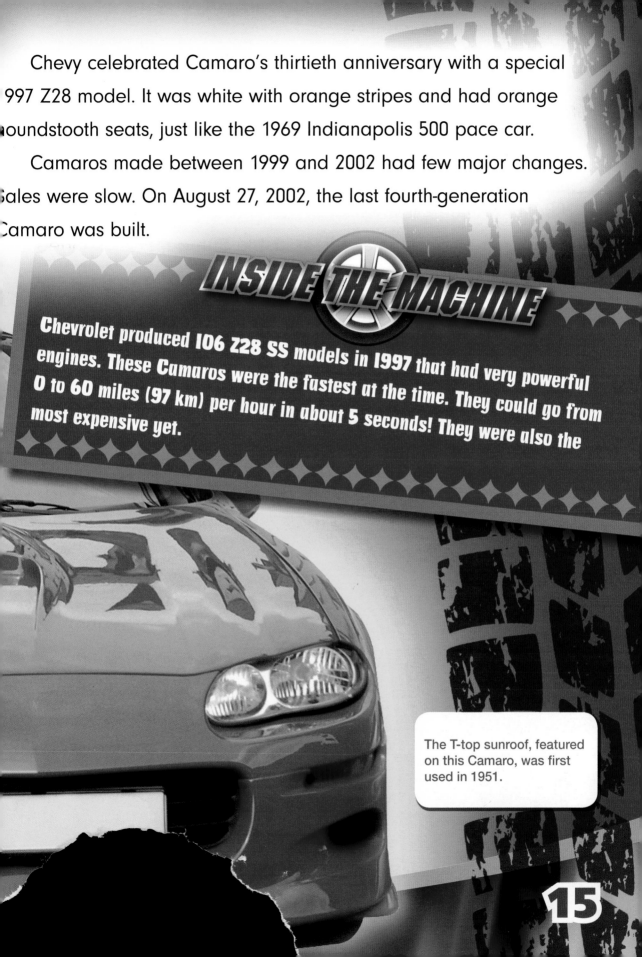

Chevy celebrated Camaro's thirtieth anniversary with a special 1997 Z28 model. It was white with orange stripes and had orange houndstooth seats, just like the 1969 Indianapolis 500 pace car.

Camaros made between 1999 and 2002 had few major changes. Sales were slow. On August 27, 2002, the last fourth-generation Camaro was built.

INSIDE THE MACHINE

Chevrolet produced 106 Z28 SS models in 1997 that had very powerful engines. These Camaros were the fastest at the time. They could go from 0 to 60 miles (97 km) per hour in about 5 seconds! They were also the most expensive yet.

The T-top sunroof, featured on this Camaro, was first used in 1951.

Fifth Generation (2010 and Beyond)

Camaro fans had to wait several years for a new model. In 2006, they cheered when Chevy featured a **concept car** at the North American Auto Show. At last, a fifth generation of the Camaro was in the works! However, people had to wait a few more years to get behind the wheel.

This 2010 Camaro SS blends past design with current automotive technology.

The 2010 Camaro SS honors the 1969 model with a similar design, especially the style of the hood and grille. Of course, this car can really go! The 2010 SS has a powerful engine and could be the fastest Camaro ever made. Camaro fans know their favorite car is back in the game.

1969 Camaro SS

INSIDE THE MACHINE

The 2010 Camaro nicely represents GM's global teamwork. The original design concept was created in the United States. The engineering ideas were shared by workers in Australia and the United States. The cars are manufactured in Oshawa, Canada.

Magnificent Muscle Cars

Muscle cars are midsize cars made in the 1960s and 1970s. All have lots of power and speed. They usually come straight from the factory ready to zoom. They have a powerful engine to make that possible. Of all the Camaros, only the SS and Z28 models are defined as muscle cars.

In December 1966, Chevy sped right into the muscle-car rivalry. Their Z28 was made just to race in the SCCA Trans Am racing series. It was sold to the public because the race's rules required it.

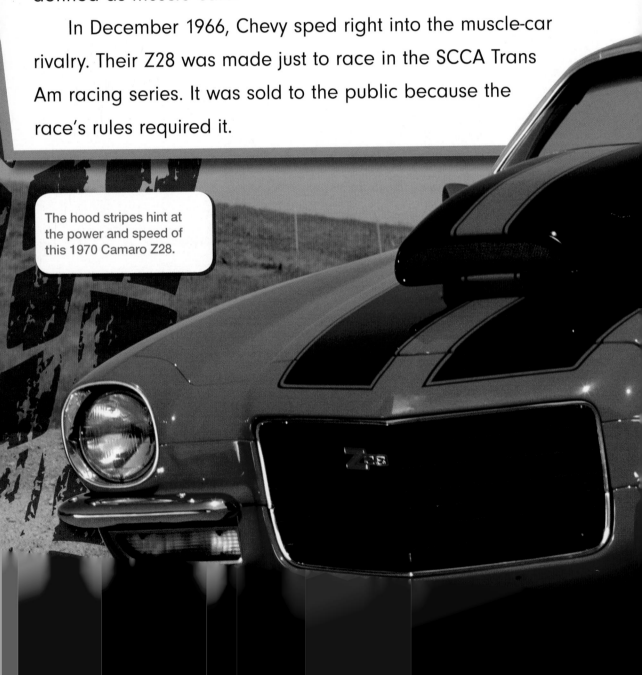

The hood stripes hint at the power and speed of this 1970 Camaro Z28.

In the first year, Z28s looked like the less powerful Camaros. There weren't even any Z28 labels on the car! However, they did have racing stripes, or wide stripes on the hood and trunk.

Hot Rods

What makes a hot rod different from a muscle car? Car fans often argue about the details. A muscle car comes from the factory with a lot of power. A hot rod is usually an older car that has been rebuilt, or "souped up," to make it go faster. Today, hot rods are displayed at car shows, but sometimes they're raced.

This 1972 Camaro SS/RS was built the last year Chevy used the special muscle-car engines called "big blocks."

Dale Earnhardt Jr. is a star of NASCAR (National Association for Stock Car Auto Racing) and the son of racing legend Dale Earnhardt Sr. He owns an excellent example of a late-model hot rod—a 1972 Camaro. Even the stainless steel bolts of his bright orange car are souped up!

INSIDE THE MACHINE

Dale Earnhardt Jr. wanted his 1972 hot rod to be fast and slick, but it has other extras, too. It has a top-of-the-line stereo for playing his favorite driving tunes. This hot rod even has a covered shelf for when Earnhardt's dog Killer comes along for the ride!

Dale Earnhardt Jr.

Start Your Engines!

Chevy kept Z28s on the track for years. In the late 1960s and early 1970s, race-car owner Roger Penske and his driver Mark Donohue won many races in their Camaros. In 2010, Camaro owner Chris Duncan and his driver Alex Hossler were American **Drag Racing** League Pro Extreme points leaders on two continents!

Not all Camaros on the track are in the actual races. In 1967, a Camaro was the pace car in the Indianapolis 500. Camaros returned to the race as pace cars five more times (1969, 1982, 1993, 2009, and 2010).

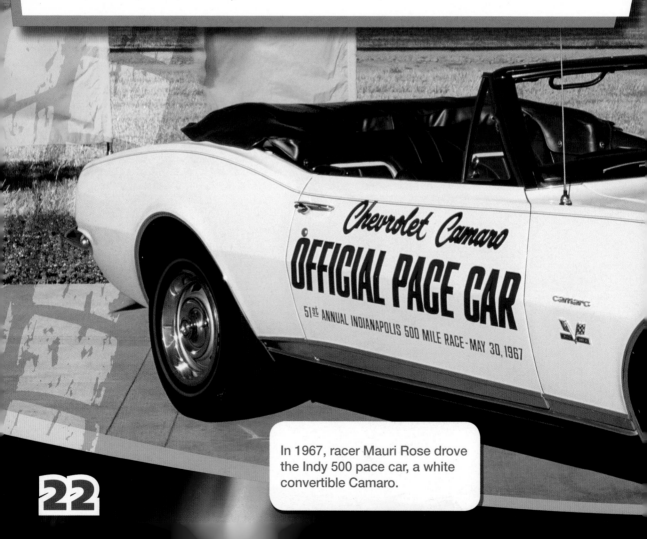

Chevrolet Camaro
OFFICIAL PACE CAR
51st ANNUAL INDIANAPOLIS 500 MILE RACE- MAY 30, 1967

In 1967, racer Mauri Rose drove the Indy 500 pace car, a white convertible Camaro.

INSIDE THE MACHINE

When Dale Earnhardt Sr. was made a member of the NASCAR Hall of Fame, Chevy offered a special Dale Earnhardt Chevrolet Hall of Fame (HOF) Camaro. It was black and candy-apple red with silver stripes. Each wheel displayed the number 3—the number on Earnhardt's racing cars. Only ten of these special Camaros were made!

Dale Earnhardt Sr.

Stars and Their Cars

Plenty of famous people drive around in fancy cars, but some really have a passion for their wheels. Late-night TV talk-show host Jay Leno actually has a Camaro named after him! It's called the Jay Leno Camaro SEMA 2009. SEMA means Specialty Equipment Market Association. The Leno Camaro SEMA has a special grille that is only featured on this Camaro.

First-generation Camaros, such as this 1967 SS, are prized by muscle-car fans.

24

Chef Guy Fieri is another loyal Chevy driver. He travels in a bright red 1967 Chevy Camaro SS convertible on his Food Network TV show *Diners, Drive-Ins, and Dives.*

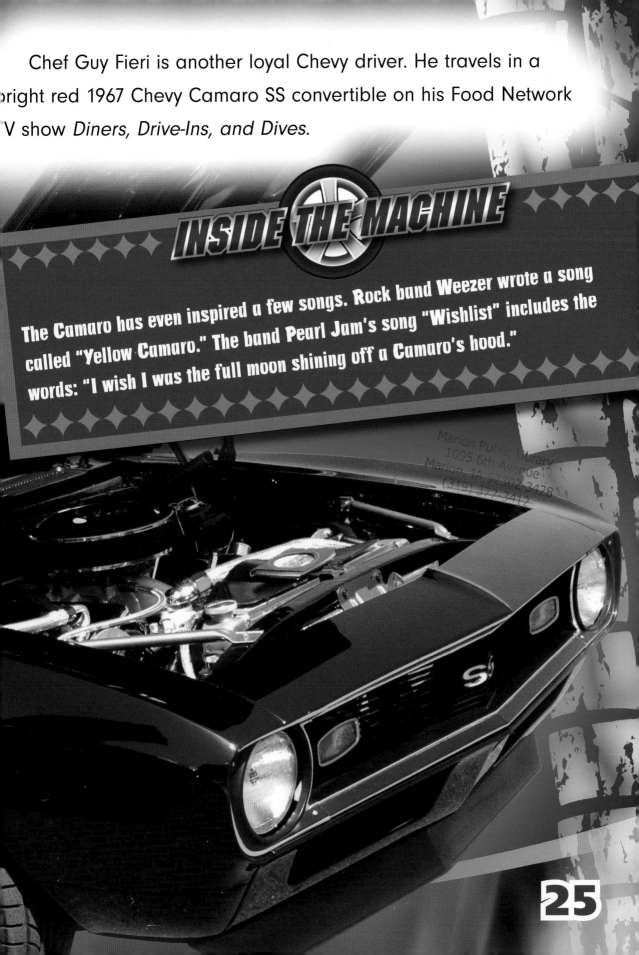

INSIDE THE MACHINE

The Camaro has even inspired a few songs. Rock band Weezer wrote a song called "Yellow Camaro." The band Pearl Jam's song "Wishlist" includes the words: "I wish I was the full moon shining off a Camaro's hood."

Yellow Camaro on the Silver Screen

Plenty of Camaros have appeared in movies. General Motors presented a concept car for the 2007 movie *Transformers*. The yellow car with black stripes starred as "Bumblebee." It had a new look in the second *Transformers* movie in 2009. It created a buzz with lots of Camaro fans!

This is the 2007 Camaro used in the first *Transformers* movie.

Many people wanted to zip down the highway in their own yellow and black Camaro, so Chevy announced a 2010 special edition model. This head-turning car is fitted with special details. It has a shield on the door that mirrors the symbol of the Autobots, the group of good robots in the movie.

Drew Barrymore

INSIDE THE MACHINE

In the 2000 movie *Charlie's Angels*, Drew Barrymore played a Camaro-driving private detective. Her ride was an original 1969 SS convertible in the style of a 1969 Indianapolis 500 pace car in classic white with orange stripes. Chevy built fewer than 4,000 models of this pace car.

Speeding into the Future

Camaro is on a roll, winning World Car Design of the Year for 2010. An unusual feature that could take off in the years to come is gull-wing doors for the SS. These doors open up and out. They look like the wings of a gull!

A 2011 Camaro became available with a power boost. Camaros could be racing their old rival—the Mustang—in NASCAR's top league, the Sprint Cup Series, by 2013. Who knows what road Chevy Camaros will take in the future? They're sure to be racing forward!

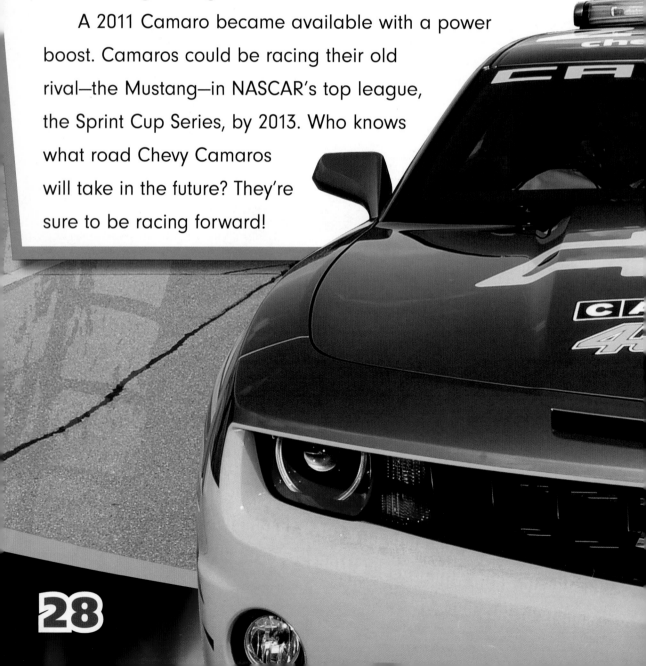

INSIDE THE MACHINE

A specially made 2010 Camaro **SS/RS** is known as the **WD-40/SEMA** Cares Camaro. It was sold to raise money for charities. This yellow and blue Camaro has been featured at car shows such as the **L.A. Auto Show.** It even shows up in the online racing game Nitto 1320 Legends.

This Camaro pace car kicked off the Carfax 400 at the Michigan International Speedway in 2009.

Glossary

concept car: a car built to show a new design and features that may one day be used in cars sold to the public

convertible: a car with a roof that can be lowered or removed

coupe: a two-door car with one section for the seat and another for storage space

design: the pattern or shape of something

drag race: a speed race between two cars with special bodies and engines on a straight track for a distance of 1/4 mile (400 m)

fender: any of the corner parts of the body of a car, especially those that surround the wheels

grille: a metal screen on the front of a car that allows cool air into the engine

houndstooth: a cloth design made up of small check-like marks

muscle car: a sports car with a powerful engine built for speed

pace car: a car that leads racers around the track to warm up their engines but does not join in the race

pony car: a small, affordable car with a sporty image

sedan: a car with front and back seats, two or four doors, an enclosed body, and a permanent top

shock: a device, such as a spring, used on a car to reduce the shaking from uneven roads

suspension: a system of springs and other devices on a car that reduces the shaking and bumping caused by uneven surfaces

For More Information

Books

Bradley, Michael. *Camaro*. New York, NY: Marshall Cavendish Benchmark, 2010.

Newhardt, David. *Camaro*. Minneapolis, MN: MBI Publishing and Motorbooks, 2009.

Wheeler, Jill C. *Camaro*. Edina, MN: ABDO Publishing, 2004.

Web Sites

Camaro
www.chevrolet.com/camaro
Keep up with the latest Camaro models and news on the Chevrolet Web site.

Collisionkids.org
www.collisionkids.org
Learn about cars by playing games and completing related projects.

NHRA: Championship Drag Racing
www.nhra.com
Keep tabs on points for your favorite Camaro racers and a lot more racing news as well.

Index